AMAZING WINTER OLYMPICS

CURLING

BY ASHLEY GISH

CREATIVE EDUCATION • CREATIVE PAPERBACKS

Published by Creative Education and Creative Paperbacks
P.O. Box 227, Mankato, Minnesota 56002
Creative Education and Creative Paperbacks are imprints of
The Creative Company
www.thecreativecompany.us

Design by The Design Lab
Production by Rachel Klimpel
Art direction by Rita Marshall
Printed in the United States of America

Photographs by Alamy (Action Plus Sports Images, Sam Mellish, PA
Images, REUTERS, Sport in Pictures, Xinhua), Getty Images (Dick
Darrell/Toronto Star), iStockphoto (Valdas Jarutis), Shutterstock
(Alexey Layeroff, ronstik, sommthink)

Library of Congress Cataloging-in-Publication Data
Names: Gish, Ashley, author.
Title: Curling / Ashley Gish.
Series: Amazing Winter Olympics.
Includes bibliographical references and index.
Summary: Celebrate the Winter Games with this high-interest intro-
duction to curling, the team sport known for its rocks and brooms.
Also included is a biographical story about curler Anna Hasselborg.

Identifiers:
ISBN 978-1-64026-493-9 (hardcover)
ISBN 978-1-68277-045-0 (pbk)
ISBN 978-1-64000-623-2 (eBook)
This title has been submitted for CIP processing under LCCN
2021937772.

First Edition HC 9 8 7 6 5 4 3 2 1
First Edition PBK 9 8 7 6 5 4 3 2 1

Table of Contents

Curling was among the 16 events included in the first Winter Olympic Games in 1924. Great Britain won the gold medal. All the players on that team were from Scotland. The sport began there long ago.

Athletes from 16 countries took part in the 1924 Winter Olympics in Chamonix, France.

Olympic curling stopped after 1924 until it was added back to the Games in 1998.

Curling is a team sport. Two teams compete against each other. Each team has four players. They play on an ice rink. Teams take turns sliding **rocks** across the rink. They try to make the rocks stop in the **house**.

house a large target on a curling rink

rocks polished granite stones used in curling

The granite used for making curling rocks comes from two places in Great Britain.

Rocks are made from granite. Each one weighs about 44 pounds (20 kg). All players use **brooms**. Many curlers wear special shoes. These help players slide and stop on the ice.

brooms also called brushes, these are used to sweep ice in curling matches

Curlers have to be patient and make smart plans as they play.

Each player on a team throws two rocks. The **skip** is the team's captain. The other players are called the lead, second, and third. Players give the rock a gentle turn as they throw it. This makes the rock **curl**.

curl to move in a curve rather than a straight line

skip a curling team's captain; the skip tells the other players where to slide their rocks

Players sweep the ice in front of the rock with their brooms. This makes the rock glide farther. It also keeps the rock from curling too much. Curling is called "the roaring game" for the rumbling sound the rock makes as it slides.

Indoor curling rinks have "pebbled ice" to help the rock grip the playing surface.

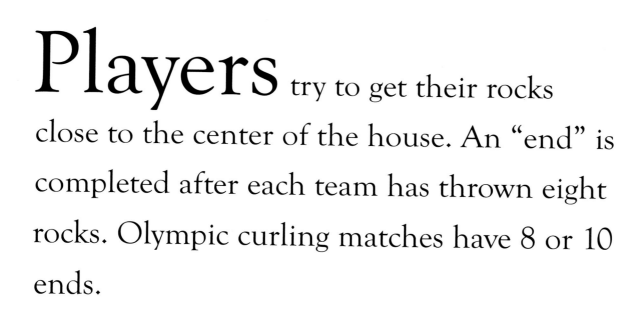

Players try to get their rocks close to the center of the house. An "end" is completed after each team has thrown eight rocks. Olympic curling matches have 8 or 10 ends.

As of 2021, Canada had the most medals in Olympic curling events.

A team earns points when its rocks are closest to the house's center. The team with the most points wins the game.

Teams try to knock their opponent's rock away from the house to keep them from scoring.

Players respect each other. They honor the rules and traditions of curling. Players try to be humble, kind, and fair both on and off the ice.

Players note their own mistakes, so there is little need for referees in curling.

Curling is fun and safe for all ages. People do not need to spend a lot of money on gear. Watch this amazing sport during the next Winter Olympics. Or try it for yourself!

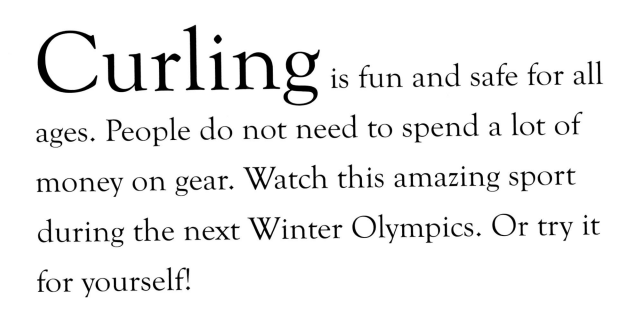

Each pair of curling shoes includes a "gripper" and a "slider" for moving on the ice.

Competitor Spotlight: Anna Hasselborg

Anna Hasselborg

is from Stockholm, Sweden. Her family loves curling. Her father, brother, uncle, and cousin are also curlers. Some of Hasselborg's favorite childhood memories involved sliding around on the ice. But this skip worked hard to get to the Olympics. She and her team from Sweden won gold at the 2018 Winter Olympic Games in Pyeongchang, South Korea.

Read More

Hunter, Nick. *The Winter Olympics*. Chicago: Heinemann, 2014.

Labrecque, Ellen. *Curling*. Ann Arbor, Mich.: Cherry Lake, 2018.

Waxman, Laura Hamilton. *Ice Hockey and Curling*. North Mankato, Minn.: Amicus, 2018.

Websites

KidzSearch: Curling
https://wiki.kidzsearch.com/wiki/Curling
Learn the basics of curling.

Paralympic.org: Wheelchair curling
https://www.paralympic.org/pyeongchang-2018/wheelchair-curling
Learn more about the Paralympic Winter Games.

Index